EFFECTIVE TEACHER INTERVIEWS

How do I hire good teachers?

Jennifer L.
HINDMAN

ASCD   Alexandria, VA USA

Website: www.ascd.org
E-mail: books@ascd.org

www.ascdarias.org

Printed in the United States of America. Cover art © 2014 by ASCD. ASCD publications present a variety of viewpoints. The views expressed or implied in this book should not be interpreted as official positions of the Association.

ASCD LEARN TEACH LEAD® and ASCD ARIAS™ are trademarks owned by ASCD and may not be used without permission. All other referenced trademarks are the property of their respective owners.

PAPERBACK ISBN: 978-1-4166-1994-9   ASCD product #SF115042

Also available as an e-book (see Books in Print for the ISBNs).

Library of Congress Cataloging-in-Publication Data

Hindman, Jennifer L., 1971-
  Effective teacher interviews : how do I hire good teachers? / Jennifer Hindman.
     pages cm
  Includes bibliographical references.
  ISBN 978-1-4166-1994-9 (pbk.)
1. Teachers--Selection and appointment--United States. 2. Employment interviewing. I. Title.
  LB2835.25.E55 2014
  371.12--dc23
                        2014029821

_____

23 22 21 20 19 18 17 16 15 14   1 2 3 4 5 6 7 8 9 10

EFFECTIVE TEACHER INTERVIEWS

How do I hire good teachers?

How Do I Start? 1

How Do I Find Good Applicants? 9

How Do I Construct a Better Interview? 13

How Do I Plan for the Interview? 25

How Do I Train a Team to Conduct Fair,
Legal, and Effective Interviews? 30

How Do I Leverage the Interview Experience? 34

How Do I Retain a New Hire? 41

Encore 45

References 50

Related Resources 54

About the Author 55

How Do I Start?

When a teacher position opens, consider what your students and school need the new hire to know and be able to do. Think of the teacher selection process as an investment in your school's success. We'll start with the research to make the process efficient and effective and then you'll be able to transfer what you're doing and learning from one interview to the next. Keep in mind that an instructional leader hires many individual teachers—decisions that matter greatly to the achievement of students and will cost the school system millions of dollars. That money is well spent when effective teachers are selected. *Effective Teacher Interviews* empowers instructional leaders to positively affect student learning through intentional selection of teaching faculty.

So how do you find good teachers? Despite the far-reaching ramifications of any hiring decision, I found that 73 percent of U.S. principals weren't trained by their school systems in how to conduct fair, legal, and effective interviews (Hindman & Stronge, 2009). Many just borrowed their interview questions from other administrators. Of course, professional collaboration is fine if the questions are good, but disastrous if they are poorly constructed or contain impermissible inquiries. In my research, mostly in the discipline of applied psychology and, to a lesser degree, in K–12 literature, I discovered how to refine the teacher interview to get better outcomes and will guide you through the process of writing and conducting an effective, legal interview.

Briefly we will explore related topics of recruitment, evaluation, performance interviewing, and retention. Also, knowing what the effective teacher research says is important to constructing a valid and reliable interview and assessing the quality of the interviewees (see James Stronge's *Qualities of Effective Teachers*, 2007). The goal of this volume, however, is to help you create an effective interview by learning how to do these five tasks:

1. Apply teacher selection research and interviewing best practices to your school's interview process

2. Develop meaningful interview items and avoid questions that are not legally permissible

3. Select and train an interview team

4. Match candidates' skills and experiences to your school's needs

5. Get the most from your interview time

With budgets tight, you can use the hiring process to improve your school without writing a single plan or sending staff to professional development. When hiring a teacher, instructional leaders possess the opportunity to select someone with the knowledge, skills, and abilities that complement their staff and initiatives (Donaldson, 1990). A well-constructed interview solicits information from the interviewee about the glows and blows of past performances. I recommend that you address the four research-based interview facets when you write the interview questions. A star

☆ next to an item indicates the best practice identified in the research literature for its specific purpose.

Facet 1: Write Good Questions

What gets asked gets answered. How interview items are phrased influences the response given. If you ask a candidate about high-yield instructional strategies, he or she can tell you about them; however, if you really want to know how well or if an interviewee has used those strategies, the item or question needs to be written differently. Researchers have examined and determined which question types most effectively predict future job performance. Four types of questions are described:

1. *Opinion questions* are good for assessing how an interviewee works with other teachers and for assessing the interviewee's ability to communicate; however, assessing the response is highly subjective. An example, "What is your teaching philosophy?"

2. *Fact questions* are knowledge or skill-based with right and wrong responses. They do not necessarily inform an interviewer of whether the interviewee knows what to do with the information. During a science teacher interview, a fact question is, "What are MSDS?"

3. *Situational questions, also called hypothetical questions*, are better than fact or opinion questions. The question provides a situation from which the applicant is to respond. The notable pitfall is that situational questions may be answered too generally or in exhausting detail.

For example, "What would you do if a parent came to your classroom multiple times in a two-week period for impromptu conferences before and during school?" The experienced and effective applicant knows that there are many "ifs" in addressing a situation and the tendency is to give either a broad encompassing response or a detailed longer response. If a candidate has never encountered a particular situation, he can still answer the question because he will know what you want to hear. Situational questions are good at measuring job knowledge (Levashina, Hartwell, Morgeson, & Campion, 2014). This type of question asks applicants what they would do in a situation and is effective at soliciting job knowledge (Conway & Peneno, 1999).

✩ 4. *Experienced-based questions, also called past behavior questions,* are an effective way to learn information about job experiences and therefore predict future job performance. For example, "Share with me how you addressed a situation when a colleague was late in giving you a contribution that was needed to meet a deadline." This kind of question encourages applicants to share their experiences (Ellis, West, Ryan, & DeShon, 2002). The way the question is phrased evokes responses that provide evidence of teacher quality and the experienced-based wording makes it more difficult for a candidate to use preconceived responses (Hanson, 2009). Assuming that the interview and employee evaluation are aligned and used by knowledgeable and trained personnel, the validity of this kind of question is high. When interviewers' ratings of candidate responses were compared with supervisors' ratings of employee performances, the correlations were statistically significant (Conway & Peneno, 1999; Huffcutt, Weekley, Wiesner, DeGroot, & Jones, 2001; Krajewski, Goffin, McCarthy, Rothstein, & Johnston, 2006; Pulakos & Schmitt, 1995; Taylor & Small, 2002).

Facet 2: Determine Criteria for Good Answers

Thinking through and defining criteria for rating interview responses is part of the planning process. Although interviewers may use several ways to assess the quality of responses, here are a few common practices:

1. In the *self-determined* approach, the interviewer only has questions with no defined means of recording the quality of the response. Whether to note the content of the response or to record anything is left to the interviewer.

2. In the *quick checks* approach, the interviewer indicates if a response is great, good, OK, or poor by checking a box. There is no criteria for assessing the response.

☆ 3. A *behaviorally anchored rubric* provides a common continuum for multiple interviewers to assess the quality of a response.

I recommend using a four-level rubric so that there are two levels to indicate acceptable responses that meet or exceed expectations and two levels for weaker responses that need improvement or are unsatisfactory. A three-level rubric consisting of unacceptable, acceptable, and target could work as well; the key is to evaluate the responses (Clement,

2007). A rubric serves to reduce an interviewer's bias and subjectivity in rating the response (Campion, Palmer, & Campion, 1997).

Keep in mind that a single rating of the overall interview or interviewee can be easily skewed. The interviewee's response to an initial question that would rate either very high or very low may influence the overall rating. If the question is answered well, the interviewer may subconsciously look for the good in all subsequent responses. Conversely, if the first response is poor, the interviewer may subconsciously try to validate that initial negative impression. To address this problem, interviewers need to rate the response to each question individually prior to asking the next item. This practice allows the interviewer's focus to move from one response to the next with as much objectivity as possible.

A rubric establishes specific criteria for each level of response and allows interviewers to focus on assessing desirable qualities. Further, a rubric supports interviewers who are not familiar with a particular content area or specialty to better assess responses. For example, a study comparing interview ratings given by special education administrators and ratings given by principals who did not have special education backgrounds found the ratings to be comparable (Ebmeier, Beutel, & Dugan, 2010). A strength of rubrics is that their use reduces variability among raters (Hanson, 2009). Further, using a defined rubric to evaluate responses helps interviewers focus on the job-relatedness quality of the response instead of applicant-specific factors, such as ingratiation techniques (e.g., flattery), an annoying voice, or a great outfit (Levashina et al., 2014).

Facet 3: Provide Note-taking Space

The research into the usefulness of note-taking and how it affects interviews shows some findings that support note-taking and other findings that are inconclusive. Interviewers often take notes and there are good reasons why. Different studies have found that taking notes (1) increases procedural accountability (Brtek & Motowidlo, 2002); (2) is often focused on applicants' behavior (Burnett, Fan, Motowidlo, & DeGroot, 1998); and (3) assists with recall of interview information (Macan & Dipboye, 1994; Middendorf & Macan, 2002). Here are the three obvious options for note-taking during an interview:

1. Take notes,
2. Do not take notes, or
☆ 3. Choose whether to take notes.

The group that chose whether to take notes had better recall than those participants in the other two groups (Burnett et al., 1998). Ideally, interview notes paraphrase what the applicant said or capture direct quotes. Some interviewers use exclamation points, stars, smiley or frowny faces, or question marks in their notes; however, when the interview day is over, most interviewers cannot remember what compelled them to make the mark. Given that interview documents, including notes, should be kept on file for several years, it is much better to have specific information. If you choose to write notes, avoid making judgments and focus on communicating what the applicant said. It is extremely helpful to record specific examples for later reference.

Facet 4: Establish the Level of Structure

The structure of an interview influences the information you can learn. Studies have examined how much structure is optimal for an interview to be predictive of future job performance and how much structure is needed to be a guard against discrimination during hiring. The following three levels of structure have been studied:

1. *Unstructured interviews* are similar to playing a pick-up football game. The game unfolds without a series of plays to run. Interview questions may not be written and, if they are, they may not be used. An unstructured interview is great for getting to know a person, building rapport, and providing a strong indication of how the candidate interacts with others.

2. *Semi-structured interviews* have a framework of key ideas or questions to ask. It is a format that is responsive to exploring a divergent path, yet allows the interviewer to refocus discussion as needed.

☆ 3. *Structured interviews* provide each interviewee with the same series of questions, giving equal opportunities to share information about their work experiences. Although interviewers may probe for additional information, they do not prompt for better answers. Structured interviews have higher validity scores than semi-structured interviews (Campion et al., 1997; Conway, Jako, & Goodman, 1995;

Levashina et al., 2014; McDaniel, Whetzel, Schmidt, & Maurer, 1994) mostly because the questions are predetermined. An analysis of complaints to the U.S. Equal Employment Opportunity Commission (EEOC) found that structured interviews were more legally defensible than less structured interviews (Williamson, Campion, Malos, Roehling, & Campion, 1997). Principals reported that their hiring decisions were best with a structured interview (Bourke & Brown, 2014). In addition, structured interviews allow you to plan questions that align to the major and vital job responsibilities.

Now that you have background on what the interview research says, consider how you will use it to inform your professional practice. Use the time when applicants are applying for your open position and to construct your interview (see p. 13).

How Do I Find Good Applicants?

Most of your potential interviewees will come from the efforts made by the human resources (HR) department. Communicate anticipated job openings to HR so they can look for suitable candidates at job fairs and as applications come in. It is one thing to say "Mrs. Snow is retiring, and we need a 7th grade teacher." It is quite another to officially notify HR that your school needs "a middle school science-endorsed teacher who can demonstrate expertise in integrating nonfiction reading and writing opportunities into problem-based learning labs in the classroom."

Seek Applicants from Human Resources

The HR department will likely post the teacher position on the school system website, relevant listservers, and physical job sites. Many professional teacher organizations have career centers on their websites where, for a fee, school systems can post openings to target applicants with particular qualifications.

HR is committed to securing viable applicants to enhance the teaching and learning in the schools they serve and they often involve building-level leadership in recruitment. One HR director sends principals to recruit for specific openings at job fairs where the district has found similar successful candidates. For example, if a principal has an opening for a teacher of special education, that principal is asked to attend a corresponding job fair and collect résumés. Upon return, the principal reviews the résumés and ranks the candidates. The HR department follows up with candidates at the top of the list to ensure that they complete the online applications, including all required attachments, and then schedules screening interviews.

Recruit Additional Applicants

As a school leader, your efforts should complement the work being done by the HR department. Obvious strategies include recruiting from within your building by notifying great substitute teachers, preservice teachers, and paraprofessionals about job openings. Also, consider how to connect with colleagues—especially if they have a reduction-in-force policy that may result in nonrenewable contracts for outstanding first-year teachers. Networking with colleagues may yield a strong early-career applicant from a neighboring school district. Consider tweeting about job openings on the school system site. Reach out to college connections and share your school's prospective needs.

Make First Impressions Matter

Your school and current faculty can be assets in the recruitment process if you consider how your ambassadors (faculty and staff) communicate about the school. Take a few moments to consider how you all influence other people's impressions of your school.

- What's your school's curb appeal? What first (and lasting) impression does your school make on visitors?
- How are applicants and community members welcomed when entering the front office? Is there an inviting place to sit and wait?
- What does your faculty say about the school?
- What methods and venues do you use to celebrate achievements?
- What does your school's digital presence convey?

Raise awareness among your faculty and staff about how their actions and words shape perceptions of the school.

Your faculty makes connections with potential applicants at professional conferences, in their neighborhoods, at community sports events and other activities, and through impromptu introductions—perhaps to a friend's nephew who is graduating and planning to teach. Positive and encouraging messages about school climate, trust, respect, leadership, colleagues, and students are powerful networking tools.

Coordinate efforts to present a positive public relations picture because potential employees are likely to do online research. Perhaps you'll choose to tweet about school happenings, your technology integration specialist will keep the school web page current, and the PTA will maintain the school's Facebook page. Send images or story ideas to the local paper (consult school district policy) so there is positive press about your school's innovative teaching or fun spirit events.

The benefits of these positive interactions go beyond applicant recruitment because they communicate with your stakeholders and the larger community. Be aware of how others perceive your school and your leadership—it all matters.

Manage the Applicant Pool

Your HR department will probably use credential screening to identify and remove unqualified applicants and incomplete applications from consideration. Otherwise a trained staff member may sort the applications by recording the knowledge, skills, and abilities found on each application or résumé. Use a spreadsheet software program or make a simple table on a sheet of paper. Any prescreening efforts enable you to focus on the candidates whose knowledge, skills, and abilities best align with the position.

Using real criteria to prioritize applications is particularly prudent when response is high for one or more positions. For example, a school system posted one art teacher position and received more than 200 applications. They were able to screen the applications to a reasonable number by determining what knowledge, skills, and abilities (KSAs) were highlighted in the posted position description and eliminating applicants who lacked many KSAs. By looking for specific data, district personnel can identify candidates who have the minimum qualifications, as well as many preferred KSAs, so that principals can decide which candidates to interview.

How Do I Construct a Better Interview?

You can use the position description to help determine the content of the interview questions. Highlight or make notes about the key functions in the position description so that you can ask interviewees to tell you about their relevant experiences. Many schools or districts have one general position description that is used for all licensed teachers.

Occasionally I find descriptions by school level; rarely do I see specific content or specialty-area descriptions (e.g., algebra teacher). For each position, customize the key knowledge, skills, and abilities that the successful teacher will need.

For example, 20 years ago, algebra was taken by high school freshmen as either an honors or a regular class. Now, high-achieving middle school students take algebra for high school credit. The impact is that strong math students are not in high school algebra classes, placing a premium on algebra-endorsed teachers who can work effectively with struggling math students as well as those who are algebra ready. For example, you could ask, "Share with me what instructional strategies and other professional actions you have found to be effective in working with struggling algebra students."

Investigate the Job Description

Use the job description to identify key components of the position. Although some descriptions only state the requirement for a current teaching license, most are one to two pages long and list the required knowledge, skills, and attributes the applicant must possess. If the position description is too brief, you will need to generate a list of the key components the candidate would need to successfully perform in the position.

Identify Themes. Read through the position description and reflect on the themes. It may be helpful to look at your school's evaluation system to identify the themes and then match them with corresponding responsibilities in the position description. The connection is valid because both the position description and the evaluation system are based on job responsibilities. Then you can review the position description to mark each item to ensure that it is captured within the themes. For example, South Carolina (ADEPT, n.d.) articulates four domains for teachers in its evaluation: (1) planning, (2) instruction, (3) learning environment, and (4) professionalism. In contrast, Virginia has seven standards including one that explicitly addresses student performance, as well as assessment and communication (VDOE, 2011). South Carolina and Virginia simply organize qualities of effective teaching differently. Ideally, every responsibility and requirement in the job description can be sorted into one of the themes found in your evaluation system.

As a final step in reviewing the job description, consider if anything is missing. If what's missing is job-relevant, such as a particular initiative in your school, add it to your themes or make a note to address the item within a theme. If your school has a growing population of English language learners, you will want to ask applicants about their experience teaching these students.

You will have to go beyond gathering themes from the job description to begin writing the interview questions. Even a quick search on the Internet will yield hundreds of sites that suggest questions for any given position. Some questions will sound good, others won't, and many are repeats. Keep in mind that your applicants are searching for questions as well. If you create your own interview questions, you will be able to avoid canned responses from your interviewees and find a teacher who will be a good fit for the position and your school.

Know What a Good Protocol Looks Like

Start getting ready for the interview by envisioning what an effective interview protocol can look like. Figure 1 shows a single interview item that synthesizes the four facets stated earlier. The figure introduces a format that synthesizes the information that the interview team will need during the interview. A template is available as Figure 2 in the Encore section. Using this format, a page for each interview question or item to be discussed, you'll have the opportunity to organize the order of your interview items by job-related themes (identified from the job description or elsewhere). Insert the theme on the line after Teacher Quality Area/ Theme. The prompt is written as an experienced-based question (see Facet 1) with a related list of sample quality indicators. These quality indicators cue the interviewers about common responses to the question. The team members may use the space available for writing notes (see Facet 3) about the candidate's response. Finally, the behaviorally anchored rubric is given to help the interviewer to assess the quality of the candidate's response (see Facet 2). Using the same item with all applicants makes this an interview with structure (Facet 4).

Examine the Interview Construction

Assess your current interview practices. Pull out documents from a recent interview and the associated

FIGURE 1: **Example of an Interview Item**

Teacher Quality Area/Theme: Assessment

Prompt: Think of a test you constructed. First, tell me about the assessment's construction and second, how you know that it accurately measures your students' learning?

Sample Quality Indicators	Notes		
• Discusses valid and reliable assessment, may mention systematic and random error			
• Identifies the curriculum, instruction, and assessment connection			
• Table of specifications			
Unsatisfactory	**Growth Area**	**Proficient**	**Exemplary**
The applicant's response has significant concerns about how to construct a valid and reliable assessment.	The applicant describes a reasonable test construction process; however has limited connection to student learning.	The applicant discusses how a valid and reliable assessment was constructed and student performance analyzed.	In addition to meeting the proficient response. . . The applicant connects the instruction and assessment components, articulating how they aligned to the curriculum.

Source: Format from Stronge & Hindman (2006), p. 50.

position description and identify the themes. For example, themes for a teacher position typically include classroom management, instruction, assessment, planning, professionalism, and communication. Most likely these are also the domains in your teacher evaluation system.

Are all interview items distributed across the themes? Review each question and identify the theme that it best aligns with. Do all your questions have content validity? Do they adequately sample the key areas identified in the position description? If so, pat yourself on the back. You have already done better than principals who intended to ask about each important part of the job, yet rarely asked about assessment and had an overrepresentation of classroom management items (Perkins, 1998). If you have holes, you now know how to fill them.

Are all questions job-relevant? Evaluate your questions for bona fide occupational qualifications (BFOQ). In other words, every question needs to be job-related. If it is not, eliminate it. Next, read the questions again to ensure that questions do not discriminate on the basis of gender, race, religion, genetics, age, or disability. For example, it is appropriate to state that the physical education teacher's job requires lifting up to 40 pounds and to ask all applicants if they can meet that requirement. However, it is inappropriate to ask that question of only certain applicants, such as those who appear to be older than 40 and out of shape.

How are your questions worded? If your questions are phrased to get the applicant talking about experiences, you are using best practices (see Facet 1). Studies find a relationship between this type of phrasing and evaluation ratings (Huffcutt, Roth, & McDaniel, 1996; Pulakos & Schmidt, 1995). You are asking the right kind of questions if you are starting your questions with these phrases:

- Tell me about a time when . . .
- Explain to me how you . . .
- Share with me an experience you had . . .

Do you use the same question set for all interviewees for the same position? If you do, that indicates fair treatment of all applicants and can reduce the likelihood of an EEOC violation (Facet 4). If you do not use the same question set, is it because you sometimes probe for more information or rephrase an item? Then you used a semi-structured interview which is also good practice. If you do not use the same questions for the same position, there is cause for concern because you cannot demonstrate equal treatment of your applicants.

Revise Questions or Write Anew

You'll need to consider whether you should revise your interview questions or start over. Neither is a daunting task.

- Do you lack interview questions for a particular position?
- Do the questions you use elicit the information you need to make a good hiring decision?
- Do you have concerns about your questions or behaviors?

- Are your questions legally sound and well-representative of the job functions? Are they worded as fact or opinion items? Consider rephrasing them as experienced-based inquiries. (Skip to Step 3.)
- Are you asking about past behaviors related to teaching and exploring all the themes identified in the position description, but need a common way to assess the applicants' responses? (Skip to Step 5.)

Write Interview Questions

Five steps are recommended for the process of writing effective interview items. You can reproduce the template in the Encore section (Figure 2) and simply write or type the items. My trick is to write using a spreadsheet so I can later use the mail merge function of my word processing program to put the interview questions or items into the order I want. For example, the top row lists the following headings: themes, question, sample quality indicator 1, sample quality indicator 2, sample quality indicator 3, unsatisfactory, growth area, proficient, and exemplary. Beneath each header, I write potential ideas that can be eventually sorted into the proper order and placed in the interview format. So, write in stages and engage in a cycle of writing and revision.

Step 1: Research what questions need to be asked. A little research can help you write interview questions from scratch. Use a copy of the job description to align your questions to the actual job responsibilities. In addition, solicit input from job-alike colleagues. For example, librarians are hired on teacher contracts, evaluated with the teacher system, and often interviewed with questions appropriate for classroom teachers, but the best qualifications for librarians are not the same as for teachers. An inquiry to a media specialist will likely result in information about the American Association of School Librarian standards where you can find information about structuring the job description.

Step 2: Determine How to Weight Themes. Identify which themes are most important to the position. Themes of instruction, assessment, and knowledge of students are usually prioritized higher than communication and professionalism. Write more questions about the important themes and ensure you address each one. For the building-level interview, plan for two to four items per theme. By having multiple items for a theme, you'll get a stronger sense of the candidate's qualifications. The candidate should answer items in the same theme with a similar level of competence.

Step 3: Write the Questions. Consider the questions you need to write by considering the information you are trying to elicit.

1. What is the purpose of your question?
2. What information are you seeking?
3. Can you get the information from somewhere else (e.g., application)? If no, then continue. If yes, then go to that source for the information instead of seeking it in the interview.

The key is for the start of the question to cue candidates to talk about themselves. Use these or other sentence stems to start the discussion in the right direction.

- Describe how you . . .
- Explain how you . . .
- Give me an example of when you . . .
- How do you . . .
- Share with me what you have . . .
- What have you done when . . .
- Tell me about a time when you . . .

Consider how the questions provide an opportunity for candidates to tell you about their experiences related to the following common themes.

1. Planning—How have you incorporated what the students do within your lesson planning process?

2. Instruction—Describe a time when you departed from a planned lesson to capitalize on a teachable moment. How did you resume the focus on the original objectives?

3. Assessment—Share the ways in which you provide formative feedback to your students.

4. Learning Environment—Describe how you have created a print-rich environment that connects to your students' work.

5. Professionalism—Explain how you have contributed to the professional growth of others.

6. Student Achievement—Tell me how you use data to create and document a particular student learning goal.

Did items 2 and 4 cause you to pause as you read them? They model the hanging question technique in which a few words are added to the end of the behavior-based item to focus the candidate on addressing the part of the item that often goes unanswered, yet can be critical in assessing effectiveness (Murphy, 2012). It is a way to focus on the decision-making aspect of the item.

When you have generated a list of questions, take the opportunity to review and revise them. Make a list of questions and a separate list of themes. Ask someone already performing the position or a job-alike peer to read over the questions and (1) indicate which theme the question best aligns with, and (2) provide feedback about the questions. Expect this activity to take about a minute per question. In addition, solicit the peer's perception of how the questions cover the job responsibilities and ask if there are any items you should add.

Step 4: Sample Quality Indicators. The sample quality indicators may be drawn from best practice, research literature, the writer's tacit knowledge, or input from an exemplary employee serving in a similar position. Indicators serve to jump start the interviewer's brain about what is commonly heard in a good response to a question. Do not use the indicators as a checklist of required talking points—a candidate certainly could have an appropriate response that is not included.

Step 5: Behaviorally Anchored Rubric. In writing the rubric to be used in assessing the candidate's response to a question, the challenge is to make each level distinct and yet flexible enough to accommodate myriad responses. I recommend a four-level rubric so there is no middle ground for rating a response. Interviewers must decide if the response rates as unsatisfactory or needs improvement or if it is proficient and meets or exceeds expectations.

Consider starting with the extremes. What would be contained in an unsatisfactory response? This is for a response so poor in quality that it seriously calls into question whether the applicant has a chance of being offered the job. Then go to the other extreme. What items are in a response that is extremely good or perhaps great? Work toward the middle of the rubric. For a proficient rating, what is contained in a good solid response? Likewise, a growth area rating describes responses where improvement and/or growth could be made—perhaps an inexperienced candidate needs time to learn the job or would benefit from on-the-job training.

Determine the Order of the Interview Items

Pay careful attention to the order in which you will ask the interview questions. Every interview protocol has items that are easy to answer. A question that is hard to answer may be technically difficult or may ask for information that the candidate is unlikely to share without first establishing a level of trust with the interview team. Yet, interview time is a finite resource. Ask an easy and expected question early in the interview as it often puts applicants at ease. If questions are related in content and scaffold off each other, ask them in an order so that the thought process continues. Put more difficult questions at the end of the interview.

How Do I Plan for the Interview?

Interviews are opportunities. They are an opportunity for two or more people to gather for the specific purpose of learning how well a potential hire might benefit the school, as well as for the applicant to gather more information about the position and organization. Interviews are about people.

With the interview questions in hand, it's time to plan the interview. Consider who will be involved, how communications will be handled, and where and when the interview will take place. Know where a particular interview fits within the hiring process. For example, some school systems have screening, building level, performance, and central office interviews in which the applicant pool is reduced at each level. The reality is that interviews take time and personnel resources, so learn about the process to achieve as much efficiency as possible.

Select an Interview Team

At a minimum, the applicant and interviewer are engaged in the interview. The number of interviewers, however, may fluctuate depending on several factors. For a screening interview, a single interviewer will do. For a building-level interview where a possible hiring decision may be made, involving a panel of three to five interviewers is beneficial, especially if the team includes a job-alike peer with the principal and another instructional leader. Leaders often have a broad sense of what is needed to do the job while an employee performing in the role or similar role has specific insights. Including teachers as interviewers communicates to the applicant that the organization values the opinions of their teachers. In addition, it provides the applicant with a familiar face if hired.

Determine the Timing

When estimating the length of the interview, consider both the number of items and the nature of those items. For a series of queries, multiply the number of questions by 3 to get the number of minutes and add about 10 minutes. For an interview with 12 questions, allow about 45 minutes for the interview (36 minutes for questions plus 9 minutes for the opening and closing of the interview and applicant questions). Interviews could be scheduled one per hour to allow time between interviews for recording or clarifying interview notes.

If an interview question or item has multiple parts, however, you'll need to add more time. Once you create the interview, do a dry run with a colleague answering the questions to get a better sense of the time needed and how to tweak the phrasing to get the information you want.

Choose a Forum

Interviews are often by telephone, web-based conference, or face-to-face. A premium is placed on face-to-face interviews, yet a screening interview could be done by phone, Skype, or another web-based technology. Telephone interviews have been found as predictive of future job performance as face-to-face interviews (Schmidt & Rader, 1999). Once the forum is determined, try to use it for all interviews to ensure equal and fair treatment of applicants for the same position. For example, a web interview offers visual information that can be used to make inferences about race, ethnicity, and age that may increase or decrease a candidate's chances for a job offer. In reality, however, applicants may encounter a prospective employer in multiple ways, including prior work with the school (e.g., parent volunteer), job fairs, or e-mail inquiries. Although it is ideal to use the same forum for all candidates, it may not be feasible. Here are three forum considerations.

- **Telephone interview.** Conduct the interview in a room free of distractions. It is more difficult to actively listen without nonverbal inputs, so remove any temptations to multitask. If multiple people are involved in the interview, use a boundary microphone. Speaker phones make it difficult for the remote person (usually the applicant) to hear anyone except the person sitting closest to the phone.

- **Web-based interview.** A webcam and a variety of free websites as well as commercial software offer interview options if travel is not viable. Typically, the actual applicant and interviewers are viewed on screen, but in some cases an avatar may be used. Visual impressions affect interview ratings in that more attractive applicants typically get better ratings, whether the visual is that actual candidate or an avatar (Behrend, Toaddy, Thompson, & Sharek, 2012). When using technology, consider the disadvantages such as dropped calls, poor Internet connections, and a field of view that restricts nonverbal cues.

- **Face-to-face interview.** The most common form of interview requires adequate space and comparable seating for everyone. Ensure that the applicant's chair does not put her at a disadvantage. If using multiple interviewers, seat the applicant where she can easily make eye contact with each team member. If possible, provide clear entry into the room.

Prepare Communications

A short e-mail message or quick phone call to each potential interviewee opens the opportunity for dialogue and makes a connection. Plan the information you need to share by making a checklist of key points or by sending a "form letter" e-mail message so that the same information is shared with each candidate. The initial contact is designed to communicate interview-related information and indicate that the organization is interested in the applicant. Consider the following specific communications to the candidate that may be preplanned:

1. *When contacting applicants for an interview.* In addition to date, time (start and end), and place (including directions), let candidates know if anything else is expected (a portfolio, a list of references, or a skills test). Use a

checklist or e-mail message to ensure objectivity, clarity, and consistency.

2. *When interviewing candidates.* During the interview you will use the interview questions listed, but you should also plan what you will say to begin and end each interview. For example, at the end of the interview, be prepared to tell applicants the next step in the process and to give an estimate of when they should hear from the organization.

3. *When announcing the results of the interview.* After the interview, use prepared messages to communicate the outcome of the interview to each candidate (i.e., job offer or not). This may be done by the HR department. Interviewers may want to send a more general e-mail message that says, "Thank you for speaking with me today. If you have any questions, please contact me at [phone number or e-mail address]." A middle school principal shared that she prepares a basic message for the job-alike interview team member to send to the interviewees. She uses this personal touch or "edge" from a peer to help persuade applicants to join her team.

Employees who are serving on the interview team need to be kept in the loop of communications. Send them the date, time, and location information as soon as possible. When you arrange release time for employees to participate in interviews, you are communicating that you value the individual's expertise. Also remember to arrange for the time they need for training and for reviewing applicants' materials before the interview.

How Do I Train a Team to Conduct Fair, Legal, and Effective Interviews?

With the interview planned, applications arriving, and the interview team identified, it is time to train the team members. A meta-analysis of 120 studies found that interviewer training had the strongest relationship to interview validity (Huffcutt & Woehr, 1999). Yet, the research shows that to conduct interviews with experienced-based questions, the interviewers need training, practice, and preparation (Barclay, 2001). In addition, they need training to decode nonverbal behaviors if that information is to be useful in selecting a good candidate (Burnett & Motowidlo, 1998). Training the interviewer has wide ranging benefits that include the ability to conduct interviews that are considered legal (or at least not illegal), to collect pertinent and job-related information, and to enhance inter-rater reliability (Stevens, 1998). To make the best hiring decisions and to help ensure the candidates are involved in fair and legal interviews, interviewer training is essential.

Plan the Training Session

Train everyone who will be in contact with the applicants. Naturally, different levels of contact will necessitate different levels of training. The person who answers the telephone inquiries should have standard answers to questions such as "What should I bring to the interview?" The secretary who greets the applicant needs to know not to ask an obviously pregnant candidate when the baby is due. And, interview team members need to know that what happens during the interview stays with the interview committee—no matter how good, shocking, or humorous.

Essential Training. Time is a resource and coordinating multiple schedules is a challenge. If you only have the time before the first interview of the day with your team, briefly discuss what knowledge, skills, and abilities the ideal candidate would have, let them read over the interview questions, and remind them of confidentiality. Make your team aware of how they may be influenced by first impressions, which are not always accurate as people may be nervous. For example, research says that based on the words you use and the sound of your voice, people make assumptions about your education level and intelligence (Hudley & Mallison, 2011). Conclude by establishing common understandings with the team (see p. 33).

Preferred Training. If your team hasn't done an interview together or with this format, try scheduling about two hours for training and application review. A 75-minute training session for the interview team, followed by reading and reviewing the materials submitted by each interviewee, can work well. A training session could include the following items:

- Interview Research—Give team members an opportunity to share good and bad interview experiences. The conversation offers the leader a preview of the issues and insight into participants' knowledge related to hiring practices. Consider using a T-chart labeled "what works" and "what doesn't work" (10 minutes).

- Hiring Process Overview—Explain how the hiring process works for your school, articulate the role of the interview team members, and state how their input will be used (5 minutes).

- Design an Ideal Applicant—Initiate dialogue about the knowledge, skills, and abilities the candidate should demonstrate and should not demonstrate. As a group, record the items on two lists (3 minutes). Ask the team to place a check mark next to the items that are outstanding and circle items that are "deal breakers" (1 minute). Then have a discussion about both sets of attributes (15 minutes).

- Interview Questions—As a group, read the interview questions (and note assigned questions) and rubrics, discuss anticipated responses, and share how a typical interview progresses, from greeting the interviewee to concluding the interview. Include a quick synopsis of what to ask, what not to ask, and how to probe for more information (25 minutes).

- Legal Considerations—Remind participants of key legislation related to hiring (e.g., in the United States, there can be no references or questions about age, gender, race, ethnicity, religion, disability, genetics, or sexual orientation). Then present a series of questions that are legal, illegal, or in the gray area for participants to practice identifying if each is BFOQ and therefore legal and appropriate to ask (15 minutes).

• Confidentiality—Emphasize that what occurs during the interviews and in team discussion may only be discussed within the team (5 minutes).

• Application Review—Read and review the résumés and other application materials from the candidates who are scheduled for interviews (minimum of 5 minutes per candidate is needed to read the application, résumé, and reference letters).

Establish Common Understandings with the Team

Communicate your expectations of the interview team, from confidentiality to how you want them to participate in the interview. For example, does the lead interviewer do all the talking or do you want team members to pose assigned questions? Remember that what is asked, is answered, and past performance is predictive of future job performance. The team should be familiar with the interview format and questions before participating in the interview. Team members need to know how to conduct a fair, legal, and effective interview. All questions, including follow-up probes, should be BFOQ (i.e., job-related). Responses to questions should be evaluated for their content and delivery. Follow-up inquiries to a response should probe for more information instead of leading an applicant to a better response.

Interviewers need to understand and agree that the interview is confidential. In other words what occurs in the interview stays with the interview team. This is even true when the interviewee

- Appears phenomenal and a team member is excited (instead, talk up the interviewee after the teacher starts working for your school).
- Shares really odd, yet funny information.
- Shares scandalous information (alas, unless there is a legal obligation to disclose information such as abuse, team members' tongues are bound).

The team also needs to know its role in the teacher selection process. Is it a team decision or will each team member's feedback be considered independently for the principal to decide? Communicating expectations prior to the start of the first interview honors the team's involvement.

How Do I Leverage the Interview Experience?

The interview is an opportunity to exchange information and make impressions. Although you cannot control if an interviewee is nervous, excited, or confidently poised, you can plan and conduct an interview to extract details about knowledge, skills, and abilities to determine suitability for the position. In executing the interview, you are capitalizing on the work that has already been done, including screening credentials, designing questions, and planning the interview.

Conduct the Interview

On the day of the interview, it is time to listen. Make sure each interviewer has a legible copy of the interview protocol and knows what to do during the interview. As the lead interviewer, tell the applicants that you want them to talk about their experiences. Every team member should communicate an interest in the applicant and should listen more than talk.

Think through what you will do if an applicant struggles with a question. Will you offer a prompt? Rephrase the question so that it is situational? Move to the next question? What do you do if you know the applicant failed the interview before it is done? For example, one candidate remarked that she drew a circle on the white board and had a misbehaving student with special needs stand with his nose touching the board inside the circle. We were appalled. We concluded the interview after asking every question, though we knew we would not hire the candidate. For the validity of the interview process, give every applicant an opportunity to respond to the same series of questions.

As an interviewer, your role is to gather data that will allow you and your team to make an informed decision. Probe applicants with a follow up question when seeking additional job-related details. Avoid prodding applicants to lead them to a better answer. In addition, remember there are multiple perspectives and a disappointed interviewee may rightfully or unadvisedly file an EEOC complaint, so treat everyone fairly. Assess responses for each item as you go.

Consider the Applicant's Perspective. The interview is an opportunity to make a positive impression on the applicant. Your best candidates likely have multiple possibilities for employment. The interviewer and applicant are both giving and making impressions. For highly desired applicants, the interview is your opportunity to recruit the candidate for your school.

A special education teacher shared that she ended an interview early because the principal was distracted. When asked why she was not interested in the position, she replied that she was very interested, but she did not want to work for someone who did not care enough about a potential staff member to stop checking e-mail messages. He tried to deny it, but then apologized as she was leaving.

Pace Your Interview Team. A marathon day of interviewing is an exhausting experience. Although there may not be time to debrief as a team between interviews, everyone can review notes and fix sloppy handwriting or type out abbreviations between appointments. If you wait until the end of the day to clarify your notes, applicants and their responses may blur together. Encourage your team members to complete their notes and the series of interviews with fidelity.

If something strange occurs during an interview, however, it is worth getting a bit off schedule to let the team process it. A workshop group told me about a candidate who was asked about his noteworthy qualifications for the job. He said that he was the hairiest man he knew. I imagine that after he left, the team needed to have a good laugh. Not all interactions are amusing. Sometimes they are stressful, especially if an applicant is negative, unprofessional, or does not seem interested in the position.

Include a Performance Interview. Performance interviewing allows applicants to demonstrate their expertise on a specific task. Examples include teaching a lesson, analyzing student data, or engaging in a virtual classroom management exercise. For example, an applicant may be given raw data and asked to provide an overview of class performance along with disaggregated data by subgroups and/or subtests in order to assess student learning. An upgrade to a writing sample is a performance assessment of a candidate's ability to communicate via e-mail message with a parent who inquired what her child could do to improve (Pappano, 2011). Essential to a performance interview is job-relatedness, task definition, and performance evaluation. Criteria to assess the performance or product submitted should be established before applicants engage in the task. Field-test the assignment with current teachers and revise as needed.

How Do I Make the Final Decision?

The selection decision involves considering all the information that has been gathered throughout the interview process. By triangulating, administrators consider what they have learned from the applicant (e.g., application, résumé, interviews), other sources (e.g., reference letters, transcripts), and recommendations from the interview team. Use what you know from your experience and the research about teacher effectiveness. John Hattie's examination of more than 900 meta-analyses uses effect sizes to illustrate the impact of various influences on achievement. Many of the top 50 influences are instructional strategies, additionally teacher credibility (#4), teacher clarity (#9), and teacher–student relationships (#12). Interestingly classroom management is #42 (Hattie, 2012), yet many interviews ask a lot of questions about it. By using multiple sources and the research to assess the candidates, the decision is based on fact, needs, insight, and expertise.

Debrief the Team. Now that the interviews are over, debrief with your team. Make connections and assessments while the applicants and their responses are still fresh in your minds. Even if all the interviews were good, it's likely that one candidate did a better job communicating her experiences, knowledge, and skills.

To narrow the field, ask each team member to (1) review his notes, (2) place applicants in order from strongest interview responses to weakest responses, and (3) put the names of the two applicants at the bottom of the list on the table face down. Typically the same two to four candidates rate low and allows the team to find common ground. As the leader, acknowledge and facilitate this agreement and suggest that, unless there are other details to be shared, the group sets these applicants aside from the discussion. The team agrees and move forward.

The agreement often increases the team's confidence in their assessment of the interviewees, making a candid discussion of the top ranked applicants richer. Depending on the number of interviewees, you may start discussing the top applicants or try steps 1 to 3 to identify the strongest applicants. (If you do this, make sure to solicit remarks about the candidates who rank in the middle. Your team may find that there is another applicant who merits discussion.) Typically, the team has consensus on the top applicants, though the order may vary. At this point, a worthwhile targeted discussion among the team can occur. When the team is finished with the discussion, collect all the interview paperwork (or save copies of PDFs) for HR.

I worked with an urban school principal who told me the interview questions were too hard for her applicants and that they rarely scored in the exemplary range. She indicated that many interviewees were new to the profession. Although we may want to hire only candidates who rate exemplary, it takes time to develop into an effective teacher. Keeping track of the experience and growth potential of your candidates is a wise reminder. The anchored rubric is simply a tool that helps you identify applicants' current knowledge and skill levels.

Until now, the assumption has been that there was a viable applicant. What do you do if none of the interviews went well? What if the top candidate takes another job and you are down to your fifth choice? Perhaps the most courageous decision is to keep looking.

Check References. Bring the top candidate's interview full circle by checking references. Keep in mind that some references may not be forthcoming with opinions for a variety of reasons. Many times, however, valuable information can be gained by picking up the telephone.

In a telephone conversation with the references, establish basic information such as how the reference knew the applicant and for how long. Ask three to five guiding questions, such as the class assignment and quality of the teacher's work, how the applicant interacts with stakeholders, and an area of professional growth the reference considers important for the applicant.

Sometimes candidates will supply reference letters instead of contact information. When reviewing these letters, note if it contains details specific to the applicant, such as:

- Explains how the letter writer is familiar with the applicant's work
- Highlights what the applicant does well
- Relates comments to the job
- Appears honest and forthcoming
- Matches gender, details, and mechanics (i.e., not a form letter)
- Provides a sense of the quality of the applicant, such as one of the top 10 percent of the teachers with whom I have worked

Archive Records. Consult your HR director for the type of records to keep, where, and for how long. The U.S.

government has rules relating to how long hiring documents must be kept and the answer varies from 1 to 2 years from the time the applicant entered the system (e.g., applied) or was hired, whichever is the later date (U.S. Department of Labor, 2010). Typical items that are kept by HR include the following:

- Copy of the position description
- Advertisements
- Records of applicants and any associated review materials, such as a credential screen
- Interview questions, as well as answers and scores
- Reference letters or notes from communications with references (e.g., telephone calls, e-mail messages)
- Signed agreement with the new hire

How Do I Retain a New Hire?

Congratulations, you made a hiring decision! Depending on the location of your school, the process likely cost from $4,366 to $17,872 in advertising and personnel costs—just to get to contract signing (Barnes, Crowe, & Schaefer, 2007). Now induction, retention, and evaluation actions matter as you work with your new employee to develop and support his or her professional growth. Retaining a teacher benefits the school district with the positive relationships built by the teacher with students and other stakeholders; the teacher's knowledge of the curriculum, school routines, and community; as well as investments in training (Brown & Wynn, 2009). In a survey of more than 4,000 Alabama teachers, 98.5 percent reported that they wanted to participate in the decision-making processes within the school and 75 percent felt empowered to make decisions (Hirsch, 2006). Engage your lead teachers in the induction and retention of their new colleague. Retaining new hires and effective teachers is a vital investment that is shared by you and your colleagues and yields resources for your school.

Plan for Immediate and Ongoing Learning

Certainly HR will have initial employee orientation information and forms for your new teacher, however, induction is a process and your leadership is needed. Many K–12 induction programs are fine during new teacher week and the teacher work week. Two weeks later, the induction experience varies wildly by school and by mentor, among other factors. If the new teacher is the only teacher in the discipline or if established groups are not welcoming, school can be a lonely place. Induction programs can help solve networking issues and the research shows that effective induction programs are required, involve mentors and administrators, provide release time, and are designed as a continuum of professional learning built on best practice and research (Webb & Norton, 2013). Involve the leadership team and key faculty and staff members in supporting the new employee in learning the school lingo, systems, and culture.

As part of the new employee training, HR typically introduces the performance appraisal process. Goal setting is a common component of performance appraisals. The purposes of goal setting vary by school and teacher, but may focus on teacher–student relationships, instructional improvement, and professional growth. Performance appraisals often use baseline performance to identify areas for improvement and to assess the results at the end of the academic year. In this case, you'll likely have an assessment of the new hire's strengths and areas for growth from the interview and application materials that can be used to inform the goal-setting process along with class baseline data. Starting a discussion on goals early in the year segues into a meaningful way for an administrator or supervisor to build a relationship with the new teacher throughout the year. Showing a commitment to the teacher, sustained interest, and discussion helps build trust.

Teacher interviews are just one investment you are making on behalf of your students, school, and school system. Teachers are motivated to meet their students' needs, engage with their jobs, and receive positive reinforcements for their efforts. As a principal, you affect the climate, morale, teacher retention, and student achievement within your school (Hindman, Seiders, & Grant, 2009). Knowing what motivates your teachers matters. When you articulate the vision for the school, build positive relationships, communicate and promote the value of students and staff to stakeholders, honor employee input, and give needed information to staff, you are developing trust and increasing teacher retention

(Dinham, 2005; Lewis, 2006; Sias, 2005). When teachers find their efforts meaningful and know that they have helped a student learn, they are motivated. They invest significant effort in designing, delivering, and assessing student learning. Recognizing their efforts, supporting their development, and valuing them in word and deed are actions that manage and increase your investment in the teacher selection decision.

To give your feedback on this publication and
be entered into a drawing for a free ASCD
Arias e-book, please visit
www.ascd.org/ariasfeedback

ASCD | arias™

ENCORE

KEY PROCESSES IN INTERVIEWING AND HIRING A GOOD TEACHER

Although creating an interview requires iterative steps, the final outcome—hiring a teacher who can be successful in your school—is well worth the effort. Here you'll find checklists that are largely chronological as a reminder of the key processes you'll use to prepare for hiring good teachers. You'll also find a blank version of the suggested interview item template that you can use to create your own effective interviews.

Reminders for the Interview Process

Get Ready

- ○ Identify the position that is needed and communicate with your HR department
- ○ Review and update the job description
- ○ Identify 4–6 themes in the job description and items you can look for during a credential screen of the application or résumé
- ○ Write effective interview items that
  - ○ Align to the position description themes and are equitably distributed
  - ○ Are all job related
  - ○ Use wording to get applicants to tell about their past professional experiences

    o Have a clear structure so every candidate is asked the same series of items for the same position

    o Contain a rubric or other framework so responses are assessed in the same way

O Provide interviewers space to write/type notes

O Offer sample quality indicators (*True confession, if time is limited to construct an interview, I skip quality indicators*)

O Solicit feedback about the interview items and revise as needed.

Get Set

O Review application materials and select interviewees

O Select an interview team of no more than five people, ideally including a job-alike peer

O Check team members' availability on the proposed interview day(s) and times.

O Compose a template for an e-mail message or a checklist to be used when setting up interviews, including date, time (start and approximate end), location with directions, information about what to bring, and a contact e-mail address or phone number for emergencies

O Train your interview team

O Provide time for your interview team to read the application materials

Interview

- ○ Arrange the interview space so the interviewee has easy access in and out of the room and is seated equitably
- ○ Remind the interview team of confidentiality, their role in the process, and how the interview will run
- ○ Provide the interview team with copies of the interview protocol
- ○ Host the interviews and pace your team
- ○ Debrief the team to get their hiring recommendation
- ○ Collect all the interview team's materials for archiving

Go

- ○ Check references
- ○ Provide your hiring decision to HR, who likely will take over the process
- ○ Thank your interview team; update them on the process, and remind them of confidentiality
- ○ Prepare for the new hire

Bonus Tip *Effective Teacher Interviews* focuses on teacher hiring. The process also works well for other positions from certified (e.g., principals, school psychologists) to classified (e.g., custodian, paraprofessional).

FIGURE 2: Template for Creating an Interview Item

Teacher Quality Area/Theme:

Prompt:

Sample Quality Indicators	Notes
•	
•	
•	

Unsatisfactory	Growth Area	Proficient	Exemplary
			In addition to meeting the proficient response . . .

Source: Format from Stronge & Hindman (2006), p. 50.

References

ADEPT. (n.d.) Performance Standards for Classroom-based Teachers http://ed.sc.gov/agency/programs-services/50/documents/ADEPT-Standards.pdf

Barclay, J. M. (2001). Improving selection interviews with structure: Organisations' use of "behavioural" interviews (electronic version). *Personnel Review, 30*(1), 81–101.

Barnes, G., Crowe, E., & Schaefer, B. (2007). *The cost of teacher turnover in five school districts: Executive summary.* Washington, DC: National Commission on Teaching and America's Future.

Behrend, T., Toaddy, S., Thompson, L. F., & Sharek, D. J. (2012). The effects of avatar appearance on interviewer ratings in virtual employment interviews. *Computers in Human Behavior, 28*(6), 2128–2133.

Bourke, K. B., & Brown, C. G. (2014). Secondary school principals' roles in employment interviews. *National Forum of Educational Administration and Supervision, 31*(3), 46–59.

Brown, K. M., & Wynn, S. R. (2009). Finding, supporting, and keeping: The role of the principal in teacher retention issues. *Leadership and Policy in Schools, 8*(1), 37–63.

Brtek, M. D., & Motowidlo, S. J. (2002). Effects of procedure and outcome accountability on interview validity. *Journal of Applied Psychology, 87*(1), 185–191.

Burnett, J. R., Fan, C., Motowidlo, S. J., & DeGroot, T. (1998). Interview notes and validity. *Personnel Psychology, 51*(2), 375–396.

Burnett, J. R., & Motowidlo, S. J. (1998). Relations between different sources of information in the structured selection interview. *Personnel Psychology, 51*(4), 963–983.

Campion, M. A., Palmer, D. K., & Campion, J. E (1997). A review of structure in the selection interview. *Personnel Psychology, 50,* 655-702.

Clement, M. C. (2007). Retention begins with hiring: Behavior-based interviewing. *Edge, 2*(5), 3–19.

Conway, J. M., Jako, R. A., & Goodman, D. F. (1995). A meta-analysis of interrater and internal consistency reliability of selection interviews. *Journal of Applied Psychology, 80*(5), 565–580

Conway, J. M., & Peneno, G. M. (1999). Comparing structured interview question types: Construct validity and applicant reactions. *Journal of Business and Psychology, 13*(4), 485–506.

Dinham, S. (2005, November). Principal leadership for outstanding schooling outcomes in junior secondary education. Presentation at the Australian Association for Research in Education, Parramatta, Australia. Retrieved October 16, 2007 from http://www.aare.edu.au/05pap/din05528.pdf

Donaldson, G. A. (1990). *Teacher selection and induction.* Reston, VA: National Association of Secondary School Principals.

Ebmeier, H., Beutel, J. L., Dugan, E. (2010). An employment interview instrument for special education teachers. *Journal of Special Education Leadership, 23*(2), 84–99.

Ellis, A. P., West, B. J., Ryan, A. M., & DeShon, R. P. (2002). The use of impression management tactics in structured interviews: A function of question type? *Journal of Applied Psychology, 87*(6), 1200–1208.

Hanson, D. M. (2009). *Principal's perceptions on the use of a teacher effectiveness interview protocol to interview and hire teachers* (Doctoral dissertation). Retrieved from Dissertations and Theses. (3385687).

Hattie, J. (2012). *Visible learning for teachers: Maximizing impact on learning.* New York, NY: Routledge.

Hindman, J. H., Seiders, A. S., & Grant, L. W. (2009). *People first: A school leader's guide to building and cultivating relationships with teachers.* Larchmont, NY: Eye on Education.

Hindman, J., & Stronge, J. (2009). The two million dollar teacher selection decision. ERS Spectrum, 27(3), 1–10.

Hirsch, E. (2006). *Recruiting and retaining teachers in Alabama: Educators on what it will take to staff all classrooms with quality teachers.* Hillsborough, NC: Center for Teaching Quality.

Hudley, A. H. C., & Mallison, C. (2011). *Understanding English variation in U.S. schools.* New York: Teachers College Press.

Huffcutt, A. I., Roth, P. L., & McDaniel, M. A. (1996). A meta-analytic investigation of cognitive ability in employment interview evaluations: Moderating characteristics and implications for incremental validity. *Journal of Applied Psychology, 81*, 459–473.

Huffcutt, A. I., Weekley, J. A., Wiesner, W. H., DeGroot, T. G., & Jones, C. (2001). A comparison of situational and behavior description interview questions for higher-level positions. *Personnel Psychology, 54*(3), 619–644.

Huffcutt, A. I., & Woehr, D. J. (1999). Further analysis of employment interview validity: A quantitative evaluation of interviewer-related structuring methods. *Journal of Organizational Behavior, 20*(4), 549–560.

Krajewski, H. T., Goffin, R. D., McCarthy, J. M., Rothstein, M. G., & Johnston, N. (2006). Comparing the validity of structured interviews for managerial-level employees: Should we look to the past or focus on the future? *Journal of Occupational and Organizational Psychology, 79,* 411–432.

Levashina, J., Hartwell, C. J., Morgeson, F. P., & Campion, M. A. (2014). The structured employment interview narrative and quantitative review of the research literature. *Personnel Psychology, 67,* 241–293.

Lewis, L.K. (2006). Employee perspectives on implementation communication as predictors of perceptions of success and resistance. *Western Journal of Communication 70*(1), 23–47.

Macan, T. H., & Dipboye, R. L. (1994). The effects of the application on processing information from the employment interview. *Journal of Applied Social Psychology, 24*(14), 1291–1314.

McDaniel, M. A., Whetzel, D. L., Schmidt, F. L., & Maurer, S. D. (1994). The validity of employment interviews: a comprehensive review and meta-analysis. *Journal of Applied Psychology, 79*(4), 599–617.

Middendorf, C. H., & Macan, T. H. (2002). Note-taking in the employment interview: Effects on recall and judgments. *Journal of Applied Psychology, 87*(2), 293–303.

Murphy, M. (2012). *Hiring for attitude: Research and tools to skyrocket your success rate* [White paper]. Retrieved June 18, 2014, from Leadership IQ: http://www.leadershipiq.com/wp-content/uploads/2012/01/Hiring_For_Attitude_1.pdf

Pappano, L. (2011). Using research to predict great teachers. *Harvard Education Letter, 27*(3). Available online only at http://hepg.org/hel-home/issues/27_3/helarticle/using-research-to-predict-great-teachers_501.

Perkins, M. Y. (1998). An analysis of teacher interview questions and practices used by middle school principals (Doctoral dissertation, Virginia Polytechnic Institute and State University, 1998). *Digital Library Archives* (URN: etd-32398-16236).

Pulakos, E. D., & Schmitt, N. (1995). Experience-based and situational interview questions: Studies of validity. *Personnel Psychology, 48*(2), 289–308.

Schmidt, F. L., & Rader, M. (1999). Exploring the boundary conditions for interview validity: Meta-analytic validity findings for a new interview type. *Personnel Psychology, 51*(2), 445–464.

Sias, P. M. (2005). Workplace relationship quality and employee information experiences. *Communication Studies, 56*(4), 375–395. Retrieved September 25, 2007 from Expanded Academic Index.

Stevens, C. K. (1998). Antecedents of interview interactions, interviewers' ratings, and applicants' reactions. *Personnel Psychology, 51*(1), 55–85.

Stronge, J. H., & Hindman, J. L. (2006). *The teacher quality index: A protocol for teacher selection.* Alexandria, VA: ASCD.

Taylor, P. J., & Small, B. (2002). Asking applicants what they would do versus what they did do: A meta-analytic comparison of situational and past behaviour employment interview questions. *Journal of Occupational and Organizational Psychology, 75*, 277–294.

U.S. Department of Labor, Compliance assistance by topic-hiring. Retrieved June 4, 2010 from http://www.dol.gov/compliance/topics/hiring-eeo-contractors.htm#recordkeeping

Virginia Department of Education. (2011). *Guidelines for Uniform Performance Standards and Evaluation Criteria for Teachers.* Richmond, VA: Author.

Webb, L. D., & Norton, M. S. (2013). *Human resources administration: Personnel issues and needs in education* (3rd ed.). Upper Saddle River, NJ: Pearson.

Williamshon, L. G., Campion, J. E., Roehling, M. V., Malos, S. B., & Campion, M. A. (1997). Employment interview on trial: Linking interview structure with litigation outcomes. *Journal of Applied Psychology, 82* (6), 900–913.

Related Resources

At the time of publication, the following ASCD resources were available (ASCD stock numbers appear in parentheses). For up-to-date information about ASCD resources, go to www.ascd.org. You can search the complete archives of Educational Leadership at http://www.ascd.org/el.

Handbook for Qualities of Effective Teachers by James H. Stronge, Pamela D. Tucker, and Jennifer L. Hindman (#104135)

The Inspired Teacher: How to Know One, Grow One, or Be One by Carol Frederick Steele (#108051)

Qualities of Effective Teachers, 2nd Edition by James H. Stronge (#104156)

The Teacher Quality Index: A Protocol for Teacher Selection by James H. Stronge and Jennifer L. Hindman (#105001)

CHILD The Whole Child Initiative helps schools and communities create learning environments that allow students to be healthy, safe, engaged, supported, and challenged. To learn more about other books and resources that relate to the whole child, visit www.wholechildeducation.org.

For more information: send e-mail to member@ascd.org; call 1-800-933-2723 or 703-578-9600, press 2; send a fax to 703-575-5400; or write to Information Services, ASCD, 1703 N. Beauregard St., Alexandria, VA 22311-1714 USA.

About the Author

Jennifer L. Hindman, PhD, is the Assistant Director of the School University Research Network in the School of Education at the College of William and Mary. She works on behalf of 28 public school systems to secure funding for and collaborate on the design and delivery of sustained professional development experiences primarily in the areas of college and career readiness, literacy, and principal leadership. Through her work with Dr. James Stronge, Dr. Hindman has facilitated the development of numerous employee evaluation processes including ones focused on teachers, educational specialists, and administrators. A former middle school teacher and science specialist, she teaches human resource management at William and Mary. Dr. Hindman is the coauthor of five books: *People First!; The Supportive Learning Environment; Planning, Instruction, and Assessment; The Teacher Quality Index;* and *Handbook for Qualities of Effective Teachers*—as well as numerous articles and grant-funded works. She appreciates the feedback from Noreen Becci, Margie DeSander, Genny Ostertag, Darcie Russell, and Angie Seiders, each of whom provided insight and perspective on drafts of this publication. Dr. Hindman dedicates this book to the teachers at Indianapolis's Mary E.

Castle Elementary School where she attended kindergarten through 5th grade. Her greatest sources of enjoyment are her husband, Barry, and their children, Miriam and Malachi. Dr. Hindman may be reached by e-mail at jlhind@wm.edu.

WHAT KEEPS YOU UP AT NIGHT?

ASCD Arias begin with a burning question and then provide the answers you need today—in a convenient format you can read in one sitting and immediately put into practice. Available in both print and digital editions.

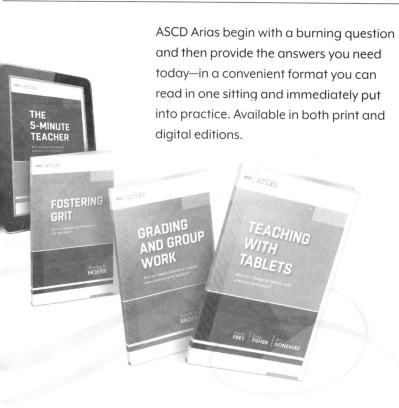

Answers You Need
from Voices You Trust

ASCD | arias™